BRAZILIAN PORTUGUESE CHIDLREN'S BOOK

COLORS AND SHAPES

FOR YOUR KIDS

AUTHOR
ROAN WHITE

ILLUSTRATIONS
FEDERICO BONIFACINI

VERMELHO

AZUL

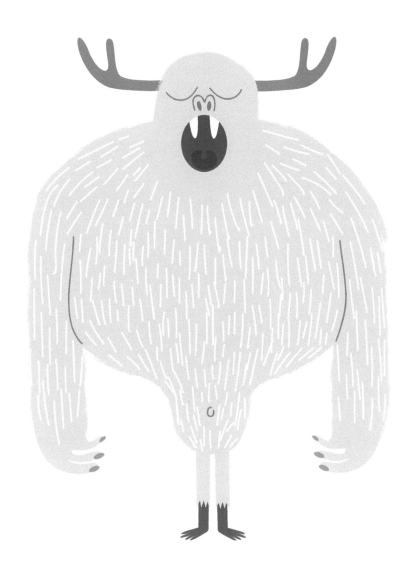

AMARELO

VERDE

LARANJA

ROXO

PRETO

MARROM

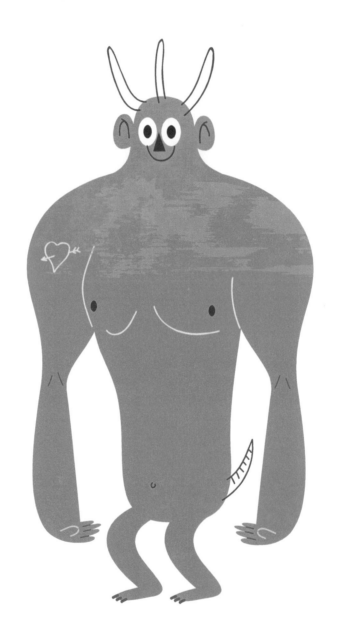

ROSA

CINZA

TRIÂNGULO

CÍRCULO

QUADRADO

RETÂNGULO

LOSANGO

PARALELOGRAMO

TRAPÉZIO

LOSANGO

PENTÁGONO

HEXÁGONO

OCTÓGONO

Printed in the USA
CPSIA information can be obtained
at www.ICGtesting.com
LVHW071022200624
783579LV00020B/54